Exam Keywords
English

Lydia Radford

Peppermint Publications Limited

Exam Keywords English

Published by Peppermint Publications Limited
95 Parc Gilbertson
Pontardawe
Swansea
SA8 4PT

ISBN 978-1-908578-09-9

Teachers' Notes

All too often students fail to do as well as they should in an exam because they have failed to answer the question correctly. They simply write as much as they possibly can to show the examiner how much they know about the subject.
Sometimes, this is simply because they don't understand the vocabulary used.
Often, the keyword in an examination question is a verb, e.g. consider, explain, identify, etc.
Exam Keywords English is a resource that aims to help students understand the vocabulary used in examination questions.
This is key to getting that higher grade.
Most of the worksheets can be photocopied and laminated and used more than once to save on printing and paper.
Each keyword could be introduced individually and studied in isolation and then introduce another keyword and so on. Once all the keywords have been introduced and discussed, start using the worksheets.
Alternatively, introduce all the keywords using the Keyword Definitions worksheet and start using the worksheets. Each student should have their own copy of the Keyword Definitions worksheet.
Make it fun. Use the flashcard worksheets at the end of this book. Copy, laminate and cut them up to make durable flashcards to use and play games. Even the brightest students enjoy playing games to learn and this provides an ideal opportunity for mixed ability group work.

Contents

Keyword Definitions

imagine	To think about something and make up how it looks or how you would feel about it.
compare	To look for and point out things that are the same and different or how far they agree or disagree with each other.
contrast	To look for and point out the differences between things.
explore	To look closely at all sides and viewpoints in order to find things out and decide what you think.
identify	To find and pick out things and make them clear.
consider	To look at and think about carefully in order to understand and decide what you think.
develop	To say more about an idea and take it further.
support	To add strength to by giving reasons for why you think something, sometimes using quotes.
list	To give a number of simple and short points in answer to a question, usually in order and with bullet points.
express	To look at the facts and put in your own words what you think, perhaps adding what might happen.
analyse	To break the text down into separate parts, looking at each idea and pointing out in detail how it has been used.
comment	To give your own thoughts and ideas about different points in the text.
describe	To give a picture in words which is well planned and gives a clear, detailed idea of what something is like.
explain	To give reasons as to why or how something happened and the effect it had.
discuss	To think about the facts of something, decide what you think and argue reasons for and against, also adding what might happen.

Matching

Link the keyword with the correct definition.

imagine	To look at the facts and put in your own words what you think, perhaps adding what might happen.
compare	To give a picture in words which is well planned and gives a clear, detailed idea of what something is like.
contrast	To add strength to by giving reasons for why you think something, sometimes using quotes.
explore	To break the text down into separate parts, looking at each idea and pointing out in detail how it has been used.
identify	To look for and point out the differences between things.
consider	To give a number of simple and short points in answer to a question, usually in order and with bullet points.
develop	To give your own thoughts and ideas about different points in the text.
support	To look closely at all sides and viewpoints in order to find things out and decide what you think.
list	To say more about an idea and take it further.
express	To look for and point out things that are the same and different or how far they agree or disagree with each other.
analyse	To look at and think about carefully in order to understand and decide what you think.
comment	To think about something and make up how it looks or how you would feel about it.
describe	To think about the facts of something, decide what you think and argue reasons for and against, also adding what might happen.
explain	To find and pick out things and make them clear.
discuss	To give reasons as to why or how something happened and the effect it had.

Choose the Correct Word

imagine	To (think/whisper/shout) about something and make up how it looks or how you would feel about it.
compare	To look for and point out things that are the same and (identical/different/similar) or how far they agree or disagree with each other.
contrast	To look for and point out the (likenesses/differences/similarities) between things.
explore	To look (briefly/closely/quickly) at all sides and viewpoints in order to find things out and decide what you think.
identify	To find and pick out things and make them (clear/complicated/similar).
consider	To look at and think about carefully in order to understand and (decide/imagine/repeat) what you think.
develop	To say more about (an idea/an object/a person) and take it further.
support	To add strength to by giving reasons for why you think something, sometimes using (questions/quotes/paragraphs).
list	To give a number of simple and short points in answer to a question, usually in order and with (paragraphs/pictures/bullet points).
express	To look at the (text/facts/pictures) and put in your own words what you think, perhaps adding what might happen.
analyse	To break the text down into separate parts, looking at each (idea/word/sentence) and pointing out in detail how it has been used.
comment	To give your (own/the author's/the examiner's) thoughts and ideas about different points in the text.
describe	To give a picture in words which is well planned and gives a (clear/simple/short), detailed idea of what something is like.
explain	To give (ideas/thoughts/reasons) as to why or how something happened and the effect it had.
discuss	To think about the facts of something, decide what you (dislike/think/like) and argue reasons for and against, also adding what might happen.

Wordsearch

q	s	d	t	y	z	e	e	b	i	r	c	s	e	d
d	p	s	o	l	k	i	x	u	y	h	n	b	g	t
t	f	d	e	v	e	l	o	p	c	d	e	s	x	q
a	r	z	x	r	f	g	h	j	l	m	n	t	b	c
v	d	o	s	w	p	t	p	y	f	a	n	q	a	t
z	x	v	p	j	j	x	l	e	l	e	i	o	o	n
q	w	e	r	p	e	d	e	n	d	b	h	n	h	e
g	a	r	s	s	u	c	s	i	d	r	e	s	s	m
b	n	e	r	t	g	s	b	g	p	p	r	h	e	m
b	a	s	d	f	g	t	h	a	j	k	o	l	r	o
n	l	f	g	h	j	k	s	m	d	h	l	x	a	c
m	y	f	i	t	n	e	d	i	s	s	p	v	p	n
l	s	c	v	b	n	h	k	k	l	y	x	e	m	e
t	e	r	e	d	i	s	n	o	c	b	e	x	o	x
t	x	v	n	l	p	t	s	a	r	t	n	o	c	r

imagine   compare   contrast   explore   identify

consider   develop   support   list   express

analyse   comment   describe   explain   discuss

Jumbled Sentences

Unjumble the words to give the correct definition.

imagine   would think feel about and make up it looks or how to you about it something how

compare   for and point things agree are out the same and or look how far to they or disagree that with each different other

contrast   out look for point things and to the between differences

explore   out look at all sides and and in think order to viewpoints things to decide closely what you find

identify   clear find to and pick things out and them make

consider   to look and think you carefully about in think to understand and at decide what order

develop   more to say an idea about and take further it

support   to to by giving reasons quotes for why you add something strength sometimes using think

list   give a of simple and short points points in answer to a to bullet usually number in order and with question

express   to at look facts the put and in own what you what might think perhaps words happen adding your

analyse   separate break the text parts at each looking and pointing to out in detail down into how it has been used idea

comment   own give different thoughts and to ideas about your points in the text

describe   give picture idea a in words well planned like a clear to detailed of gives and what is something which is

explain   had give as to reasons why happened or something how and the effect il to

discuss   think to the facts of about decide you and happen adding reasons for and what against might something also what argue think

Cloze

imagine   To think about something and make up how it looks or how you would _____ about it.

compare   To look for and point out things that are the same and different or how far they _____ or disagree with each other.

contrast   To look for and _____ out the differences between things.

explore   To look closely at all sides and viewpoints in order to find things out and _____ what you think.

identify   To _____ and pick out things and make them clear.

consider   To look at and think about carefully in order to understand and decide what you _____.

develop   To _____ more about an idea and take it further.

support   To add _____ to by giving reasons for why you think something, sometimes using quotes.

list   To give a number of simple and short points in answer to a question, usually in _____ and with bullet points.

express   To look at the _____ and put in your own words what you think, perhaps adding what might happen.

analyse   To break the text down into separate parts, looking at each _____ and pointing out in detail how it has been used.

comment   To give your own thoughts and ideas about _____ points in the text.

describe   To give a picture in words which is well planned and gives a clear, detailed idea of what something is _____.

explain   To give reasons as to why or how something happened and the _____ it had.

discuss   To think about the facts of something, decide what you think and _____ reasons for and against, also adding what might happen.

Find the Missing Word

imagine	To about something and make up how it looks or how you would feel about it.
compare	To look for and point out things that are the and different or how far they agree or disagree with each other.
contrast	To look for and point out the between things.
explore	To look closely at all sides and in order to find things out and decide what you think.
identify	To find and pick out things and make them.
consider	To look at and think about carefully in order to and decide what you think.
develop	To say more about an and take it further.
support	To add strength to by giving for why you think something, sometimes using quotes.
list	To give a number of simple and points in answer to a question, usually in order and with bullet points.
express	To look at the facts and put in your own what you think, perhaps adding what might happen.
analyse	To break the text down into parts, looking at each idea and pointing out in detail how it has been used.
comment	To give your own and ideas about different points in the text.
describe	To give a picture in words which is well planned and gives a clear, detailed of what something is like.
explain	To give as to why or how something happened and the effect it had.
discuss	To think about the of something, decide what you think and argue reasons for and against, also adding what might happen.

Multiple Choice

imagine	<ul><li>To say more about an idea and take it further.</li><li>To think about something and make up how it looks or how you would feel about it.</li><li>To give your own thoughts and ideas about different points in the text.</li></ul>
compare	<ul><li>To find and pick out things and make them clear.</li><li>To look for and point out things that are the same and different or how far they agree or disagree with each other.</li><li>To give a picture in words which is well planned and gives a clear, detailed idea of what something is like.</li></ul>
contrast	<ul><li>To look for and point out the differences between things.</li><li>To think about the facts of something, decide what you think and argue reasons for and against, also adding what might happen.</li><li>To break the text down into separate parts, looking at each idea and pointing out in detail how it has been used.</li></ul>
explore	<ul><li>To give reasons as to why or how something happened and the effect it had.</li><li>To look at and think about carefully in order to understand and decide what you think.</li><li>To look closely at all sides and viewpoints in order to find things out and decide what you think.</li></ul>
identify	<ul><li>To find and pick out things and make them clear.</li><li>To give a number of simple and short points in answer to a question, usually in order and with bullet points.</li><li>To add strength to by giving reasons for why you think something, sometimes using quotes.</li></ul>
consider	<ul><li>To give a picture in words which is well planned and gives a clear, detailed idea of what something is like.</li><li>To break the text down into separate parts, looking at each idea and pointing out in detail how it has been used.</li><li>To look at and think about carefully in order to understand and decide what you think.</li></ul>
develop	<ul><li>To look for and point out things that are the same and different or how far they agree or disagree with each other.</li><li>To look at and think about carefully in order to understand and decide what you think.</li><li>To say more about an idea and take it further.</li></ul>

support	<ul><li>To find and pick out things and make them clear.</li><li>To add strength to by giving reasons for why you think something, sometimes using quotes.</li><li>To think about something and make up how it looks or how you would feel about it.</li></ul>
list	<ul><li>To give your own thoughts and ideas about different points in the text.</li><li>To find and pick out things and make them clear.</li><li>To give a number of simple and short points in answer to a question, usually in order and with bullet points.</li></ul>
express	<ul><li>To look at the facts and put in your own words what you think, perhaps adding what might happen.</li><li>To look for and point out the differences between things.</li><li>To look closely at all sides and viewpoints in order to find things out and decide what you think.</li></ul>
analyse	<ul><li>To think about something and make up how it looks or how you would feel about it.</li><li>To break the text down into separate parts, looking at each idea and pointing out in detail how it has been used.</li><li>To look closely at all sides and viewpoints in order to find things out and decide what you think.</li></ul>
comment	<ul><li>To say more about an idea and take it further.</li><li>To give your own thoughts and ideas about different points in the text.</li><li>To look for and point out things that are the same and different or how far they agree or disagree with each other.</li></ul>
describe	<ul><li>To find and pick out things and make them clear.</li><li>To give a picture in words which is well planned and gives a clear, detailed idea of what something is like.</li><li>To look at and think about carefully in order to understand and decide what you think.</li></ul>
explain	<ul><li>To give reasons as to why or how something happened and the effect it had.</li><li>To look for and point out the differences between things.</li><li>To give a number of simple and short points in answer to a question, usually in order and with bullet points.</li></ul>
discuss	<ul><li>To add strength to by giving reasons for why you think something, sometimes using quotes.</li><li>To think about the facts of something, decide what you think and argue reasons for and against, also adding what might happen.</li><li>To say more about an idea and take it further.</li></ul>

Multiple Choice (2)

To think about something and make up how it looks or how you would feel about it.	○ Imagine ○ Contrast ○ Identify
To look for and point out things that are the same and different or how far they agree or disagree with each other.	○ Explore ○ Compare ○ Consider
To look for and point out the differences between things.	○ Contrast ○ Identify ○ Develop
To look closely at all sides and viewpoints in order to find things out and decide what you think.	○ Consider ○ Support ○ Explore
To find and pick out things and make them clear.	○ List ○ Identify ○ Develop
To look at and think about carefully in order to understand and decide what you think.	○ Express ○ Support ○ Consider
To say more about an idea and take it further.	○ List ○ Develop ○ Analyse
To add strength to by giving reasons for why you think something, sometimes using quotes.	○ Support ○ Express ○ Comment

To give a number of simple and short points in answer to a question, usually in order and with bullet points.	○ Describe ○ Analyse ○ List
To look at the facts and put in your own words what you think, perhaps adding what might happen.	○ Express ○ Comment ○ Explain
To break the text down into separate parts, looking at each idea and pointing out in detail how it has been used.	○ Describe ○ Discuss ○ Analyse
To give your own thoughts and ideas about different points in the text.	○ Imagine ○ Comment ○ Explain
To give a picture in words which is well planned and gives a clear, detailed idea of what something is like.	○ Describe ○ Discuss ○ Compare
To give reasons as to why or how something happened and the effect it had.	○ Imagine ○ Contrast ○ Explain
To think about the facts of something, decide what you think and argue reasons for and against, also adding what might happen.	○ Explore ○ Discuss ○ Compare

Name the Keyword

_____ To think about something and make up how it looks or how you would feel about it.

_____ To find and pick out things and make them clear.

_____ To add strength to by giving reasons for why you think something, sometimes using quotes.

_____ To look closely at all sides and viewpoints in order to find things out and decide what you think.

_____ To look for and point out things that are the same and different or how far they agree or disagree with each other.

_____ To look at the facts and put in your own words what you think, perhaps adding what might happen.

_____ To say more about an idea and take it further.

_____ To look for and point out the differences between things.

_____ To give a number of simple and short points in answer to a question, usually in order and with bullet points.

_____ To give your own thoughts and ideas about different points in the text.

_____ To break the text down into separate parts, looking at each idea and pointing out in detail how it has been used.

_____ To look at and think about carefully in order to understand and decide what you think.

_____ To think about the facts of something, decide what you think and argue reasons for and against, also adding what might happen.

_____ To give reasons as to why or how something happened and the effect it had.

_____ To give a picture in words which is well planned and gives a clear, detailed idea of what something is like.

Delivering Definitions

Give the correct definition for each keyword.

imagine _____

compare _____

contrast _____

explore _____

identify _____

consider _____

develop _____

support _____

list _____

express _____

analyse _____

comment _____

describe _____

explain _____

discuss _____

Keyword Examples

Circle the keyword that best suits the paragraph.

1 The adventure weekend course included:
- cycling
- caving
- kayaking
- horse riding
- climbing
- orienteering

          LIST   DISCUSS   EXPLAIN

2 The OAPs disembarked from the coach at their hotel, a five-star, newly built complex. The rooms were large and luxurious, all with en suite. The hotel had a variety of bars and restaurants and a free form swimming pool. Whereas, the school party arrived at their no-star hotel, which was old and well worn. The rooms were small and shabby and the students had to share the grubby bathroom down the hall. The 'pool' was a hot tub in the overgrown and unkempt gardens. There were no bars and restaurants at the hotel, the nearest situated in the little village, a three-mile hike down the track.

          COMPARE   CONTRAST   DESCRIBE

3 The family had to decide which place to holiday next. The holiday brochure contained two holidays they particularly liked. Both resorts were described as having excellent facilities including cinemas, a theme park and leisure complexes with fantastic water parks. The two resorts were situated on the coast with wonderful sea views and long promenades, great for leisurely walks by day or night. However, one was much cheaper but much further away from the airport.

          IMAGINE   SUPPORT   COMPARE

4 Our mental health concerns our ability to be happy in ourselves, to enjoy life, survive pain, disappointment and sadness. Consequently, we need a positive sense of well-being in order to be happy. Stress is the inability to cope with everyday life and affects our sense of well-being. Therefore, stress makes us unhappy.

          EXPLORE   EXPLAIN   EXPRESS

5 The leaflet gives top tips for a good night's sleep. They include avoiding drinks which contain caffeine. These drinks include coffee and cola. Fit some exercise into your day but not just before you go to bed. Take a relaxing bath. Dedicate your room to sleep - that means no TVs or games consoles! Get into a regular routine of going to bed and getting up at the same time.

          IDENTIFY   DESCRIBE   CONSIDER

6 I read the article on heart disease and it convinced me to do more exercise. The heart is a muscle and just like any other muscle, with exercise, it becomes stronger. Although the article seemed confident that this message was getting through to people, I'm not convinced. According to experts, many young people are spending too much time on sedentary activities, playing on their games consoles and watching DVDs.

          LIST   IMAGINE   COMMENT

7 She appeared from nowhere, a dainty, diaphanous figure, a sparkling white cloud, floating in front of me. Her skin was of the finest soft, smooth velvet and her eyes were deep blue oceans. Her hair was as delicate as freshly fallen snowflakes and as she stepped toward me, I could smell the sweet perfume of honeysuckle. I gently took her hand. She was gone.

          DESCRIBE   SUPPORT   EXPLAIN

8 According to recent data, 8,000 people in the UK are on the waiting list for an organ transplant, but less than 3,000 transplants are carried out annually. More donors mean more lives saved. It can be a wonderful gift to give someone. However, some people worry that doctors wouldn't try as hard to save people on the donor register. This is something the medical profession vehemently denies. I believe if you are prepared to accept an organ, if you needed one, and most of us would, you should be prepared to donate one.

COMPARE   EXPRESS   IDENTIFY

9 I thought about being Tom. It's the beginning of World War II and I'm on a train leaving London for Wales as an evacuee. I am terrified, sad and very alone, even though I am surrounded by hundreds of other children. I think I'm going to faint. I'm not looking forward to my unfamiliar, new home. I miss my Mum and Dad already and it was only less than two hours ago when I last saw them.

IMAGINE   CONSIDER   COMMENT

10 In Steinbeck's *Of Mice and Men*, there is an intense loyalty and friendship between Lennie and George. George looks after Lennie and in return George has Lennie's companionship and unfaltering loyalty. Further to this idea, there is a strong sense of morality, that is, we should look after others less fortunate than ourselves.

DESCRIBE   COMPARE   DEVELOP

11 In the poem, the poet employs a number of linguistic devices. He begins by using personification when he compares Death to a person. 'Death ran towards me.' He then uses the metaphor 'I am a lion' to express the soldier's bravery in the face of death. He ends the poem with a simile using alliteration, 'Fight, fight for freedom forever.'

ANALYSE   LIST   EXPLORE

12 The article looks at people's attitudes to giving money to charities. Many people are happy to give money to charities; others ask: 'Why should we give away our hard-earned money?' Maybe, because it's a good and moral thing to do. But doesn't charity begin at home? I wouldn't agree with this attitude. I believe that to have a happy well-functioning society we should help people less fortunate than ourselves. Who knows, tomorrow anyone of us could need help.

IDENTIFY   CONSIDER   SUPPORT

13 Should National Service be brought back for 19-21 year olds? Given that one in four young people are unemployed, some say, this is exactly what young people need to teach them discipline and give them a purpose. However, this assumes that all young people are indisciplined and have no purpose. I disagree. I believe most young people are well-balanced with a focus, perhaps going to university or working towards a particular career. Also, if one in four people are unemployed that means three out of four are gainfully employed or in training. I don't think National Service would be in the best interest of young people.

DISCUSS   DESCRIBE   CONTRAST

14 In the text, the impression given is of a very rundown flat. He describes it as 'squalid', 'scruffy' and 'smelly'.

DISCUSS   SUPPORT   DEVELOP

15 The article raises the question 'Should the driving age be lowered to 16?' One viewpoint suggests that if you can marry and be in employment at 16, it only makes sense that you should be able to drive. However, there are concerns that 16-year-olds are not mature enough to be in control of a potentially dangerous machine. I don't believe we should penalise all 16-year-olds for the sake of an immature minority. I think there are good reasons to lower the driving age to 16, it seems unfair to keep it at 17.

EXPLORE   ANALYSE   IMAGINE

Additional Information

Imagine

When writing your own piece of work

Use of Vocabulary	Command of language - Powerful Metaphors, similies, imagery, personification Dialogue could be humorous/funny Variety to create effects Verbs are strong e.g. terrify rather than frighten Good use of adjectives
Structure of Writing	A story that is well-planned and has detailed ideas and descriptions Use of the five senses to describe Effective paragraphs make effective description
Tone	Variety Use of humour? Serious? Emotive?
Style	Informal Detailed
Use of fact from text	Not applicable
Use of opinion from text	Not applicable
Gives own viewpoint	Talk about thoughts and feelings You can write about people, places, events or emotions
Make use of own general knowledge to add more	Draw on own experience to be able to write with confidence about your opinion Can sometimes be better to draw on something you've actually experienced
Additional features	The scene can be clearly visualised Creates its own world Original and highly entertaining Gives powerful accounts of real or imagined experiences Small details of behaviour Writing will show rather than tell
Add your own tips/suggestions for 'Imagine'	

Compare

When responding to a given text

Use of Vocabulary	Link text using connectives, e.g. However, On the other hand, Similarly, Whereas
Structure of Writing	Compare texts as you go along OR write about one text first then the other and then compare
Tone	Serious Business-like approach
Style	Formal Systematic
Use of fact from text	Yes
Use of opinion from text	Difference in attitudes
Gives own viewpoint/opinion	Look at both sides of the question objectively then in conclusion give your own thoughts Sum up with own thoughts/ideas/personal feelings
Make use of own general knowledge to add more	No
Additional features	Find ways that texts are similar and different Look for links/same themes/main ideas/key points Be systematic as you study texts in spotting similarities AND differences Look at how language/vocabulary used is different Give examples of differences, e.g. quotes Comment on: language, audience, purpose
Add your own tips/suggestions for 'Compare'	

Contrast

When responding to a given text

Use of Vocabulary	Link text using connectives, e.g. However, On the other hand, Despite, Even though, Whereas, In contrast
Structure of Writing	Contrast texts as you go along OR write about one text first then the other and then contrast
Tone	Serious Business-like approach
Style	Formal Systematic
Use of fact from text	Yes
Use of opinion from text	Difference in attitudes
Gives own viewpoint/opinion	Look at both sides of the question objectively then in conclusion give your own thoughts Sum up with own thoughts/ideas/personal feelings
Make use of own general knowledge to add more	No
Additional features	Find ways that texts differ Look for links/same themes/main ideas/key points Be systematic as you study texts in spotting differences Look at how language/vocabulary used is different Give examples of differences, e.g. quotes Comment on: language, audience, purpose
Add your own tips/suggestions for 'Contrast'	

Explore

When responding to a given text

Use of Vocabulary	Precise Make good use of your extended vocabulary
Structure of Writing	Open with a brief overview of topic to introduce theme Finish with an interesting sentence Finish with summary of the views and a final opinion
Tone	Serious Business-like approach Fair
Style	Formal Systematic
Use of fact from text	Look at and think carefully at the facts Look at evidence
Use of opinion from text	Think carefully about other people's opinions
Gives own viewpoint/opinion	Introduce a new viewpoint Look at both sides of the question objectively then in conclusion give your own thoughts Sum up with own thoughts/ideas/personal feelings
Make use of own general knowledge to add more	Draw on own experience to be able to write with confidence about your opinion
Additional features	Try to find out the truth about something Look at lots of different ideas/feelings Give different views
Add your own tips/suggestions for 'Explore'	

Identify

When responding to a given text

Use of Vocabulary	Use vocabulary from text Make good use of your extended vocabulary
Structure of Writing	Clear paragraphs stating each point Good main topic sentences to start each paragraph
Tone	Serious Business-like approach Factual
Style	Formal Systematic
Use of fact from text	Look at and think carefully about the facts
Use of opinion from text	Say whether writer effective or not
Gives own viewpoint/opinion	No
Make use of own general knowledge to add more	No
Additional features	Scan to find all points Mainly present and give facts Add further formation to make each point very clear Mention all relevant parts
Add your own tips/suggestions for 'Identify'	

Consider

When responding to a given text

Use of Vocabulary	Use vocabulary from text Make good use of your extended vocabulary
Structure of Writing	Clear paragraphs stating each point State what has happened and write your own response Finish with summary of the views and own opinion Finish with interesting sentence
Tone	Serious Business-like approach
Style	Formal
Use of fact from text	Look at and think carefully about the facts Look at evidence
Use of opinion from text	Difference in attitudes Think carefully about other people's opinions Try to understand and come to some opinion of your own
Gives own viewpoint	Look at both sides of the question objectively then in conclusion give your own thoughts Sum up with own thoughts/ideas/personal feelings Think about the implications
Make use of own general knowledge to add more	Draw on own experience to be able to write with confidence about your opinion
Additional features	Look at the information given and write about what you think
Add your own tips/suggestions for 'Consider'	

Develop

When writing your own piece of work or responding to a given text

Use of Vocabulary	Make good use of your extended vocabulary
Structure of Writing	Clear paragraphs Use good linking main topic sentences
Tone	Serious Business-like approach Fair
Style	Formal
Use of fact from text	Look at and think carefully about the facts
Use of opinion from text	Difference in attitudes Think carefully about other people's opinions Try to understand and come to some opinion of your own
Gives own viewpoint	Look at both sides of the question objectively then in conclusion give your own thoughts Sum up with own thoughts/ideas/personal feelings Write about an idea in more depth/detail Introduce alternative viewpoint
Make use of own general knowledge to add more	Draw on own experience to be able to write with confidence about your opinion
Additional features	Really extend on what has been said Add further ideas Attempt to say what might happen Attempt to say possible effects Add different slants/sides
Add your own tips/suggestions for 'Develop'	

Support

When responding to a given text

Use of Vocabulary	Use vocabulary from text
Structure of Writing	Write clear paragraphs Use quotes Use embedded short quotations in your own sentences Place long quotations (more than one sentence) in a separate paragraph
Tone	Serious Explanatory Knowledgeable Firm
Style	Formal
Use of fact from text	A good way to back up your opinions is to give facts, statistics or evidence from text Say how facts have added weight to argument
Use of opinion from text	Difference in attitudes Think carefully about other people's opinions Try to understand and come to some opinion of your own
Gives own viewpoint	Yes but only backed up with evidence from/reference to text
Make use of own general knowledge to add more	Draw on own experience, backed by evidence, to be able to write with confidence about your opinion
Additional features	To say why something is true /false Quotation marks would be used Use exact words spoken Mention/refer to someone else's thoughts/comments and put their name to it
Add your own tips/suggestions for 'Support'	

List

When responding to a given text

Use of Vocabulary	Use vocabulary from text
Structure of Writing	Bullet points Use of commas in a sentence Chronological order Short sentences
Tone	Serious Business-like approach Explanatory
Style	Formal Systematic Factual
Use of fact from text	Yes
Use of opinion from text	Yes when asked to list
Gives own viewpoint	No
Make use of own general knowledge to add more	No
Additional features	Contains examples in order Can be used to focus the reader's attention Highlight important information Information is well organised
Add your own tips/suggestions for 'List'	

Express

When writing your own piece of work or responding to a given text

Use of Vocabulary	Introduce a viewpoint using connectives - However, According to, On the other hand, Additionally, Despite this, Moreover, Firstly, Finally, Consequently, As a result, Meanwhile, Nevertheless Can make use of emotive language
Structure of Writing	Write in first person 'I' if expressing own views Detailed rhetorical questions can be used effectively Link paragraphs - the first sentence of a new paragraph can be linked to previous paragraph Finish by summarising your main viewpoint clearly
Tone	Serious Explanatory Emotive?
Style	Formal Systematic
Use of fact from text	Say how facts have added weight to argument Look at and think carefully about the facts A good way to back up your opinions is to give facts, statistics or evidence from text
Use of opinion from text	Difference in attitudes Think carefully about other people's opinions Try to understand and come to some opinion of your own
Gives own viewpoint	Look at both sides of the question objectively then in conclusion give your own thoughts Sum up with own thoughts/ideas/personal feelings Make viewpoint clear Give reasons for a point of view
Make use of own general knowledge to add more	Draw on own experience to be able to write with confidence about your opinion
Additional features	Use humour to balance strong feelings Talk about feelings in particular Use anecdotes Make point with evidence from text Link your ideas together
Add your own tips/suggestions for 'Express'	

Analyse

When responding to a given text

Use of Vocabulary	Use good standard English Link text using connectives - However, According to, On the other hand, Additionally, Despite this, Firstly, Finally, Consequently, As a result, Whereas
Structure of Writing	Clear paragraphs stating each point
Tone	Serious Business-like approach Explanatory
Style	Formal Systematic Factual
Use of fact from text	Say how facts have added weight to argument Look at and think carefully about the facts A good way to back up your opinions is to give facts, statistics or evidence from text
Use of opinion from text	Say whether writer effective or not Difference in attitudes Think carefully about other people's opinions
Gives own viewpoint	Has text achieved its aim?
Make use of own general knowledge to add more	Generally only refer to text
Additional features	Comment on use of sentences, e.g. short for dramatic effect - Get Out! Refer to a variety of literary techniques, e.g. language, metaphors, similies, alliteration Show how effective writer has been Techniques used for effectiveness, contrast, humour, anecdotes, rhetorical questions, emotive language Identify essential features, how they have been used and to what effect
Add your own tips/suggestions for 'Analyse'	

Comment

When responding to a given text

Use of Vocabulary	Make use of extended vocabulary Link text using connectives - However, According to, On the other hand, Additionally, Despite this, Moreover, Firstly, Finally, Consequently, As a result, Meanwhile, Nevertheless Can make use of emotive language
Structure of Writing	Clear paragraphs stating each point Use compound and complex sentences to give your thoughts
Tone	Serious Thoughtful Emotive?
Style	Formal
Use of fact from text	Say how facts have added weight to argument Look at and think carefully about the facts A good way to back up your opinions is to give facts, statistics or evidence from text
Use of opinion from text	Difference in attitudes Think carefully about other people's opinions Try to understand and come to some opinion of your own
Gives own viewpoint	Look at both sides of the question objectively then in conclusion give your own thoughts Sum up with own thoughts/ideas/personal feelings Give clear and firm opinions Give reasons for your viewpoint referring to text
Make use of own general knowledge to add more	Draw on own experience to be able to write with confidence about your opinion
Additional features	Comment on RELEVANT points only Say why/how something has been used and how effective it is Say how the design of a media text has been effective
Add your own tips/suggestions for 'Comment'	

Describe

When writing your own piece of work

Use of Vocabulary	Good use of adjectives Metaphors, similes, imagery, personification Command of language – powerful Variety to create effects Can make use of emotive language
Structure of Writing	Make a good plan Use compound and complex sentences to give a picture Very detailed Use of five senses
Tone	Variety Use of humour Serious Explanatory Emotive?
Style	Formal or Informal Detailed
Use of fact from text	Not applicable
Use of opinion from text	Not applicable
Gives own viewpoint	Include own thoughts/feelings
Make use of own general knowledge to add more	Draw on own experience to be able to write with confidence about your opinion
Additional features	Go there in your mind Striking introduction and conclusion Show rather than tell Aim to give a clear picture of what you are describing
Add your own tips/suggestions for 'Describe'	

Explain

When responding to a given text

Use of Vocabulary	Use explanatory phrases - As a result, This meant, This is because, The reason for this is, Consequently, Therefore, It could be, It may/might be Define technical terms Use simple literal English
Structure of Writing	Must be clear, easy to understand Well planned in logical order Clear introduction Good main topic sentence to start each paragraph Clear paragraphs stating each point
Tone	Serious Business-like approach Explanatory Knowledgeable Logical Authoritive Confident
Style	Formal Systematic
Use of fact from text	Say how facts have added weight to argument Look at and think carefully about the facts A good way to back up your opinions is to give facts, statistics or evidence from text
Use of opinion from text	Difference in attitudes Think carefully about other people's opinions Try to understand and come to some opinion of your own
Gives own viewpoint	Give reasons for your viewpoint referring to text
Make use of own general knowledge to add more	Yes
Additional features	Different from straightforward information Sets out how or why something happens Give reasons throughout Limit points, better to explain a few in more depth Present situation, say why it happened and the effect it had Make ideas very clear - give examples Show causes and effects
Add your own tips/suggestions for 'Explain'	

Discuss

When responding to a given text

Use of Vocabulary	Link text using connectives – I think, I consider, I believe, My view is, I discovered, My understanding, On the other hand, However, Firstly, Finally, Nonetheless, Alternatively Colourful Make good use of extended vocabulary
Structure of Writing	Start with punchy, opening sentence/main topic sentence A short striking sentence to end is good Use rhetorical questions
Tone	Serious Business-like approach Explanatory Fair
Style	Formal Systematic Factual
Use of fact from text	Say how facts have added weight to argument Look at and think carefully about the facts A good way to back up your opinions is to give facts, statistics or evidence from text
Use of opinion from text	Difference in attitudes Think carefully about other people's opinions Try to understand and come to some opinion of your own Balance facts and opinions
Gives own viewpoint	Look at both sides of the question objectively then in conclusion give your own thoughts Sum up with own thoughts/ideas/personal feelings Include your own opinion with each paragraph Decide what you think about the issue Add a new point to end
Make use of own general knowledge to add more	Yes
Additional features	Give reasons backed up by evidence Structure arguments in a logical way Don't rewrite question as first paragraph – make it snappier End with strong, memorable point Quote from text
Add your own tips/suggestions for 'Discuss'	

True or False

Keyword	MIGHT USE OR WRITE ABOUT……..	True False
imagine	Metaphors, similies, personification	
compare	How language/vocabulary used is different	
contrast	Similarities and differences	
explore	Different facts and opinions	
identify	Facts	
consider	The five senses to describe	
develop	Facts only	
support	References to the text	
list	Bullet points	
express	An emotive tone	
analyse	A variety of literary techniques	
comment	Every detail in the text	
describe	A striking introduction and conclusion	
explain	Short sentences	
discuss	Other people's feelings/opinions	

OTHER EXAM KEYWORDS

1.	account	A description or explanation of what has happened.
2.	advise	Writing to help someone think, say or do something.
3.	argue	To give reasons for a point of view in order to get a message across.
4.	audience	Whom you are writing for.
5.	evidence	Things known to be true.
6.	extract	Part of the text.
7.	fact	Something known to have happened.
8.	impression	How something makes you think or feel.
9.	influence	The power of the writer to make others think or feel a certain way.
10.	inform	To tell or give facts, ideas and thoughts.
11.	instruct	To teach, to tell.
12.	main idea	The most important point in a text, poem or paragraph.

13.	opinion	What someone thinks in their own mind about something.
14.	persuade	To make someone feel a certain way about something.
15.	quotes	Words used that are taken from the text.
16.	reasons	Why you think or feel something or why something has happened.
17.	refer	To look to the text when answering the question.
18.	response	What you feel or think after reading a text.
19.	review	A short description of a book, play, etc., including what you thought of it.
20.	suggest	To offer or put forward an idea, thought or opinion.
21.	suspense	To create a sense of uncertainty or tension.
22.	viewpoint	Something you feel strongly about often backed up by reasons.

Suggestions for Games/Using Flashcards

These games are ideal for use with SEN and EAL students. They can also be used successfully with all students.

These photocopiable worksheets should be laminated and cut into individual cards for use when playing the games suggested below. REMEMBER don't cut up the original master worksheets as you will need more than one set!

Many of these games can be played in small groups with a student being the caller.

- Display keywords in the classroom.
- Play card games using the keyword flashcards:
  1) Bingo. Prepare Bingo cards with about ten keywords on each card. The caller says the keyword. If the player has the keyword definition they cover the word on their card with a counter. Variations could be the caller says the definition and the player covers the keyword etc.
  2) Each player in a small group can be given 4 or 5 cards from one pack (keyword). The caller holds up a card from the second pack (definition) and says, "Who has .....?" The player with the correct card can 'lose' that card. The player who 'loses' all their cards first is the winner.
  3) Grab. Keyword cards are spread on the table face up. The caller says the keyword and the player grabs the correct card (definition) and keeps it. If the wrong card is grabbed, the player must replace all the cards they have collected.
  4) Beetle Drive. In the centre, place a picture of a beetle. Place a pack of numbered keyword cards face down next to the picture. Each player needs paper and pencil. If the player can give the correct definition for a keyword card picked up, they can draw the appropriate numbered part of the beetle on their paper. The first player to complete their picture is the winner.
  5) Snap. Can be played by matching the keyword to the keyword definition.

6) Donkey. Using a set of keywords and a set of keyword definitions, remove one keyword or keyword definition card. The players hold their cards so that their opponents cannot see them and, in turn, choose one of their opponent's cards. If it makes a pair, the player puts the pair down in front of them. If not, they put the card in their holder. The loser is the one left with the odd card.

7) Pairs. Spread out two packs of cards on the table keeping the two packs separate (keywords/definitions). The player turns over a card from one pack, then a card from the second pack. If they match, the player keeps the pair. If not, the player turns them face down again and the next player has a turn. As the game proceeds, the players should remember where specific cards are and should find it easier to make a match. The player with the most cards wins. A variation of this could be, all the cards are laid out face down on a table.

8) Laminate a keyword definition worksheet and cut each definition into strips. The teacher calls out the keyword and the player chooses the correct definition for a point. Various matching games can be played.

<u>Exam Keywords</u> English	explore
imagine	identify
compare	consider
contrast	develop

support	comment
list	describe
express	explain
analyse	discuss

Exam Keywords

English

To look closely at all sides and viewpoints in order to find things out and decide what you think.

To think about something and make up how it looks or how you would feel about it.

To find and pick out things and make them clear.

To look for and point out things that are the same and different or how far they agree or disagree with each other.

To look at and think about carefully in order to understand and decide what you think.

To look for and point out the differences between things.

To say more about an idea and take it further.

To add strength to by giving reasons for why you think something, sometimes using quotes.

To give your own thoughts and ideas about different points in the text.

To give a number of simple and short points in answer to a question, usually in order and with bullet points.

To give a picture in words which is well planned and gives a clear, detailed idea of what something is like.

To look at the facts and put in your own words what you think, perhaps adding what might happen.

To give reasons as to why or how something happened and the effect it had.

To break the text down into separate parts, looking at each idea and pointing out in detail how it has been used.

To think about the facts of something, decide what you think and argue reasons for and against, also adding what might happen.

ANSWER PAGE

Wordsearch

q	s	d	t	y	z	e	e	b	i	r	c	s	e	d
d	p	s	o	l	k	i	x	u	y	h	n	b	g	t
t	f	d	e	v	e	l	o	p	c	d	e	s	x	q
a	r	z	x	r	f	g	h	j	l	m	n	t	b	c
v	d	o	s	w	p	t	p	y	f	a	n	q	a	t
z	x	v	p	j	j	x	l	e	l	e	i	o	o	n
q	w	e	r	p	e	d	e	n	d	b	h	n	h	e
g	a	r	s	s	u	c	s	i	d	r	e	s	s	m
b	n	e	r	t	g	s	b	g	p	p	r	h	e	m
b	a	s	d	f	g	t	h	a	j	k	o	l	r	o
n	l	f	g	h	j	k	s	m	d	h	l	x	a	c
m	y	f	i	t	n	e	d	i	s	s	p	v	p	n
l	s	c	v	b	n	h	k	k	l	y	x	e	m	e
t	e	r	e	d	i	s	n	o	c	b	e	x	o	x
t	x	v	n	l	p	t	s	a	r	t	n	o	c	r

P.11

imagine – think
compare – same
contrast – differences
explore – viewpoints
identify – clear
consider – understand
develop – idea
support – reasons
list – short
express – words
analyse – separate
comment – thoughts
describe – idea
explain – reasons
discuss – facts

P.18/19

1. list
2. contrast
3. compare
4. explain
5. identify
6. comment
7. describe
8. express
9. imagine
10. develop
11. analyse
12. consider
13. discuss
14. support
15. explore

P.35

imagine   TRUE
compare   TRUE
contrast   FALSE
explore   TRUE
identify   TRUE
consider   FALSE
develop   FALSE
support   TRUE
list   TRUE
express   TRUE
analyse   TRUE
comment   FALSE
describe   TRUE
explain   FALSE
discuss   TRUE